HAMMERSMITH
& FULHAM
PAST & PRESENT

Aerial view of Fulham, *c*. 1928.

Aerial view of Hammersmith, *c*. 1928.

HAMMERSMITH & FULHAM
PAST & PRESENT

PATRICK LOOBEY

WHSmith

First published in the United Kingdom in 2002 by
Sutton Publishing Limited exclusively for
WHSmith, Greenbridge Road, Swindon SN3 3LD

British Library Cataloguing in Publication Data
A catalogue record for this book is available from the British Library.

ISBN 0-7509-3116-7

Illustrations

Front endpaper: The Broadway and Queen Caroline Street, *c.* 1914.
Back endpaper: The Broadway and Queen Caroline Street, 2002.
Half title page: Fulham parish church of All Saints, *c.* 1913.
Title page: Hammersmith Palace, Music Hall, Kings Street, *c.* 1914.

Typeset in 11/14pt Photina and produced by
Sutton Publishing Limited, Phoenix Mill,
Thrupp, Stroud, Gloucestershire GL5 2BU.
Printed and bound in England by
J.H. Haynes & Co. Ltd, Sparkford.

Contents

South Park Gardens, *c.* 1906. Perhaps the children were asked not to smile.

The Mall, Hammersmith, from Hammersmith Bridge, *c.* 1914.

Introduction

The village of Fulham has a recorded history dating back to the eighth century with a grant of land to the Bishop of London. The bishops moved into their own palace here in the fourteenth century, and the crossing of the Thames was an important factor in the development of Fulham from as early as the Neolithic period and into Roman times. A Viking army wintered here in the ninth century, probably within the moated area of the later palace grounds. The soil in Fulham was fertile and up to the beginning of the twentieth century supported numerous fruit and vegetable nurseries. Even the 1894–6 Ordnance Survey maps show wide-open spaces between the river and Fulham Palace Road, but the last few years of the Victorian era were to see the former fields torn up for housing development. This development brought with it the need for local government to look after the health and wealth of its inhabitants; sewers, drainage, hospitals and schools were quickly to follow on the heels of the house builders. Large villas lined the riverside from the seventeenth to the nineteenth century; among them were Brandenburgh House, Broomhouse and Ranelagh House. John Dwight founded Fulham Pottery in about 1671 to manufacture porcelain and stoneware articles. A kiln

The Broadway, Hammersmith, *c.* 1908.

has been left as a reminder of the business. The first bridge on the Thames above London Bridge was erected here in 1729, requiring a large payment to the ferrymen in recompense for their loss of revenue. At that time it was called Fulham Bridge but it was often referred to in the eighteenth century as Putney Bridge. The old wooden bridge was replaced with the present stone one in 1886; it was widened in 1931–3.

Hammersmith's early livelihood depended on the resources of the Thames and it was considered an outlier of Fulham parish. Hammersmith parish church, St Paul's, was first built in 1630 as a chapel of ease for Fulham parish church. The church was rebuilt in 1883. The old Roman roads, Goldhawk Road and the Great West Road, were to become the main focus for the existence of the town, providing wayfarers with hostelries and sustenance. The riverside attracted many artists from the eighteenth century onwards, among them men such as William Morris, who lived at Kelmscott House, designing his tapestries and wallpapers. The riverside also attracted industry and factories; the West London Waterworks, for example, occupied 3 acres of the waterfront until 1965. Lead mills, saw mills, brewers, distillers and Manbre & Garton's sugar refinery filled up the riverside from Fulham to Chiswick with wharves and factory buildings. The factories had largely disappeared by the end of the 1970s and today the water's edge is gradually filling up with eagerly sought-after riverside apartments.

What has been astonishing is the ease with which the modern photographer has been able to recognise the 'old' streetscapes despite the redevelopment of the late twentieth century. The sad loss of many fine and interesting buildings is to be regretted. The Granville Theatre at Walham Green was demolished in 1971 without a preservation order being granted, but at least its loss led to the immediate listing of other threatened theatres in London. Let us hope, as redevelopment continues, that no more historic treasures will disappear from Hammersmith and Fulham.

All the photographs within this book are from the collection of Patrick Loobey. Photographic copies are available from him at 231 Mitcham Lane, Streatham, London SW16 6PY. Tel: 020 8769 0072. Email: pat@loobey.co.uk; website: www.loobey.co.uk

Putney Bridge, *c.* 1906.

Fulham's Main Thoroughfares

The King's Head public house, Fulham High Street, *c.* 1914. This pub is first mentioned in 1693. The earlier building was replaced in 1884 but it had to be rebuilt in 1906 when the western side of the High Street was demolished to allow the trams through.

The Grand Theatre in Fulham High Street was built in 1897. Ellen Terry and Sarah Bernhardt both appeared here. The theatre was demolished in 1957/8 and replaced by an office block occupied by the British computer firm ICT, later ICL. The High Street is to the left of the theatre and to the right is Putney Bridge Approach. The King's Arms public house, first mentioned in the sixteenth century, was rebuilt in 1888. It lay empty for a number of years throughout the 1990s before recent refurbishment when it was renamed the Larrik. The former Temperance snooker hall on the right was also empty for about twenty years before conversion into a public house called O'Neill's.

The High Street, Fulham, *c*. 1914. It is disgraceful that so many perfectly serviceable eighteenth-century buildings in the High Street have been demolished over the past thirty years and replaced with small office blocks that no one will remember in a hundred years. Of interest is the Golden Lion public house at no. 53, dating from 1836. This replaced an earlier pub of Tudor date. What is now the Fulham Preparatory School at no. 47a was built in 1861 as the Fulham National School. The golden terracotta façade is worth a second look.

Horse-drawn buses using the small forecourt of the Greyhound public house in Fulham Palace Road as a terminus, *c.* 1906. Today The Puzzle pub, it has lost many of its architectural embellishments and now looks quite plain and uninteresting.

Another view of Fulham Palace Road, with the Greyhound public house on the left, *c.* 1914. Wills & Sons' telegraph and post office, on the corner of Greyhound Lane, has been transformed into a Sainsbury's Local supermarket.

Fulham Palace Road, with Beryl Road on the right, 1913. The Guinness Trust buildings, further along on the right and constructed in 1901, are the largest structure in the earlier view but they are now dwarfed by the vast Broadway development in Hammersmith, built in 1994.

The Rifle public house, on the corner of Distillery Lane and Fulham Palace Road, 1913. The pub was managed for about forty years by the Mancini brothers Toni and Alfred and their father. All were of boxing fame and the pub was then named the Golden Gloves. It was renamed the Suffolk Punch in about 1996. On the next corner is the Distillers Arms public house, widely known as the Distillers, in Chancellors Road, which marks the boundary between Fulham and Hammersmith.

The Fulham Infirmary in Fulham Palace Road, seen here in about 1913, was opened in 1850 as the Fulham Union workhouse. Additional wings were added in 1871 and in 1884 the new infirmary was built. The title 'hospital' was only added in 1928. The old hospital was gradually demolished from 1966 onwards to make way for the new Charing Cross hospital, transferred here from central London. The seventeen-storey building has 900 beds and ten operating theatres as well as clinics specialising in various conditions and a cancer treatment unit.

Fulham Road viewed from outside the King's Head public house in the High Street, *c.* 1907. The mechanical omnibus was just being introduced to London's streets at this time and the horse-bus had only another seven years of service before relegation to the history books. The Borough of Fulham Electricity Department notice placed on the stenchpipe in the middle of the road informs the public that its electricity for heating and lighting is available at one penny per unit.

The junction of Fulham Road and Munster Road, *c.* 1913. The small bank on the right is now a Carphone Warehouse outlet, while the Frost & Co. stores, which had a wonderful display of fruit and vegetables on the pavement, now house a Europa food and wine supermarket.

Two telegraph delivery 'boys' pose for the camera at the corner of Rostrevor Road and Fulham Road, *c.* 1914. The splendid Munster Park Methodist Chapel, on the corner of Chesilton Road, was capable of seating a thousand worshippers in 1871. It has been demolished and replaced by a three/four-storey block of offices with single-storey shops in front.

Fulham Road, with Purcers Cross Road on the right, *c.* 1914. The shopping parade on the left was built in 1894 with living accommodation above. Winchendon Road is to the left.

Dawes Road, *c.* 1906. The Bedford Arms public house is on the left. The pub was rebuilt sometime before its recent renaming as the Frog. Alongside is Bedford Passage. The pub on the right, rebuilt in the 1930s, has thankfully retained its original name as the Wilton Arms. Aintree Street is on the right.

Dawes Road, *c.* 1914. Filmer Road is on the right. The post office and bakery on the right are now a decorator's shop. The Salisbury Tavern on the corner of Sherbrooke Road on the left is another fine old pub that has lost many of its architectural features. The capitals of the false columns and the cast-iron ornamental railings below the first-floor windows have all been removed.

The tall building on the right is the White Horse public house in Parsons Green, seen here in about 1926. The pub is mentioned in the late eighteenth century but was rebuilt in the late nineteenth century. The other buildings on the right form part of Lady Margaret's Church of England School for Girls. The various properties of the school include Belfield House, Elm House and Henniker House. While taking the modern series of photographs in this area, the author's attention was drawn to several notices erected to warn of road works and alterations taking place in the Parsons Green area. One of these notices proved most amusing. It stated: 'Traffic calming and pedestrian alterations.' Who, one wonders, invited the pedestrians to be altered and what was to be done to them?

Wandsworth Bridge Road with Sandilands Road to the left, *c.* 1925. Further along can be seen the Star Kinema. Few of the shops nowadays bother with erecting the sun awnings so popular in the earlier view. The trees have grown to enormous size in the past seventy-five years.

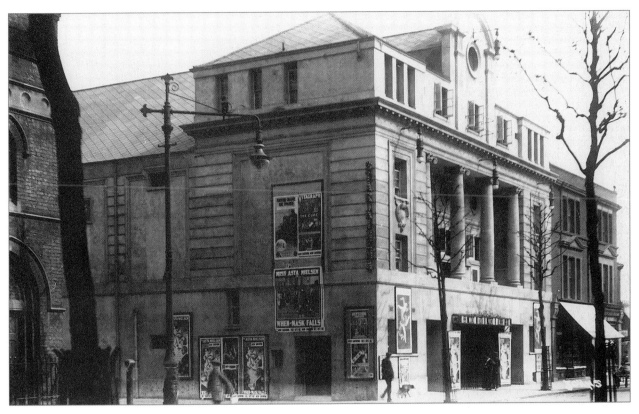

The Star Kinema in Wandsworth Bridge Road, on the corner of Broughton Road Approach, *c.* 1913. The cinema was built in 1913 with seating for 606 patrons. It closed on 4 February 1956 and was eventually demolished in 1961. The replacement building, Mirabell House, has shops on the ground floor and flats above.

The northern end of Wandsworth Bridge Road, viewed from New Kings Road, *c.* 1913. Capps Ltd wine merchants appear to be umbrella repairers as well, judging by the umbrella hanging next to the sun awning. The shopping parade facing Eelbrook Common has now been rebuilt and the former wine merchants' is now a bicycle supplies outlet called Bikepark.

The New Kings Road with Parsons Green to the left, viewed from Coniger Road, *c.* 1920. T. Wilkey's corner shop has been rebuilt and Winkworth estate agents now occupy the outlet. Bradbourne Road is to the right.

New Kings Road, with Eddiscombe Road on the left, *c.* 1908. On the corner of Cortay Road (right) W.E. Botting's fruit and vegetable store is advertising that 'You may telephone from here'. Before the introduction of public pavement-mounted telephone boxes after the First World War, members of the public had to search for outlets with one of these signs to enable them to make a call. Public pay phones were installed on pavements as early as 1911 but were not common until the early 1920s.

Walham Green

A policeman keeping watch on the traffic in Walham Green Broadway, *c.* 1925. The old village name has now been superseded by Fulham and this road is now called Fulham Broadway. In 1890 the town elders decided to build Fulham Town Hall nearby, thus setting in motion the obliteration of the name Walham Green.

Walham Green, *c.* 1925, and Fulham Broadway, 2002. Traffic lights now obscure the view along Vanston Place to the right. The central building has recently been replaced with the unimaginatively named Fulham Centre office block, which houses firms associated with the petro-chemical industries.

The Broadway, Walham Green, seen from the corner of Jerdan Place, *c.* 1912. The shopping parade on the right has been rebuilt since the Second World War. The buildings on the left had more interesting architectural details than the replacement Fulham Centre. What a pity nobody has thought of reintroducing 'Walham' into the naming of some new feature or structure in the area.

The Broadway, Walham Green, *c.* 1925. The District Railway station is on the right. The former four-storey Barclays Bank is now a Pricecheck supermarket and the former Swan Tavern to the right of the bank been renamed Bootsy Brogan's. Happily the bank retains many of its architectural embellishments, although the stone swan has gone from the roof of the pub.

The Town Hall in the Broadway, Walham Green, *c.* 1912. The smaller properties to the left of the White Hart public house were demolished to make way for the Town Hall extension. The White Hart is first mentioned in the churchwardens' accounts in 1632. The Guinness clock on the front of the pub is correct twice a day!

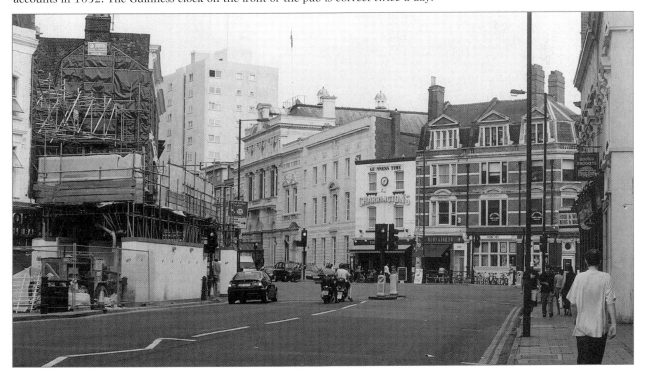

Walham Green Broadway, from Argon Mews, *c.* 1925. Note the small advertisements on the roof parapet for each shop. Phelp Brothers' printing works is to the left (now rebuilt), followed by Tyne Main Coal depot, the Broadway Dining Rooms and Lemmon's opticians, where a large pair of eyes stare out at the passers-by.

The Congregational Church in Dawes Road was built in 1887 but had to be demolished after suffering bomb damage in 1944. The replacement flats are called Mathew Court. Beyond the church is the St John's National School, which opened on 23 August 1894. The school is now the Dawes Road Adult Education Centre.

This view of Jerdan Place was taken from the rear of St John's Church, facing Fulham Road, *c.* 1913. A recent innovation is the semi-pedestrianisation of Jerdan Place, but pedestrians have to be wary of unruly cyclists. The shops on the right appear rather sad and neglected; the replacement of the rendered drip sill and the removal of the paint from the brickwork would improve their appearance enormously.

Walham Green station was built in 1880 on the District Railway and this new entrance was constructed in 1910, only a few years before this photograph was taken. The local shopkeepers finished off the old village name Walham Green in 1952, when they managed to persuade London Transport to alter the station name to Fulham Broadway. It seems that visitors were confused and couldn't find their way. Fulham village is a separate entity from Walham Green and this fact should never be forgotten. A new development to the right of the station, due to open in late 2002, will see a new Sainsbury supermarket, a Wetherspoon public house and a new station entrance almost 100 yards from the old one.

Don't rely on the old Town Hall clock in Harwood Road – it's only correct twice a day. The Town Hall, seen here in about 1905, was built in 1890 with further extensions added later. Effie Road is to the right. The HSBC bank now operates from the former London, City & Midland bank on the corner. The area has seen a proliferation of estate agents in recent years as house prices increase.

Fulham Town Hall, the administrative centre of the Borough of Fulham from 1890 to 1965, was relegated to secondary functions when the new Borough of Hammersmith and Fulham was formed in 1965 and the Town Hall in Hammersmith was chosen to serve it. The earlier view of Harwood Road, looking up to the Broadway, is from about 1912. Note the small offices built alongside the Town Hall and occupied by Foxton's estate agents.

The heart of Walham Green village, with Dawes Road on the left and Jerdan Place on the right, taken from North End Road, *c.* 1914. St John's Church was built on the site of the village pond in 1828 to the designs of J.H. Taylor. The church has been altered inside with the addition of a second floor to provide space for a community counselling service. The block of flats on the left is called Mitford Buildings.

Costermongers' stalls in North End Road, from the corner of Walham Grove, *c.* 1906 and 2002. The stalls mainly sell fruit and vegetables but today a few will be selling mobile phones, household and cleaning articles, tools and electrical goods. The costers were moved on from Hammersmith in the 1880s by disgruntled shop owners and settled in this road. Their stalls attracted trade, which encouraged house owners to alter their premises into shops, thereby attracting even more trade.

The trading outlet at 336 North End Road, on the corner of Epirus Road, could hardly be more different in 1909 and 2002. Parke's Drug Stores were part of a chain of pharmacies established across London before the First World War; they supplied a range of their own proprietary medicines and photographic materials. Dr Gull's 'Blood Purifier, Nature's Own Tonic' and 'Leibics – Meat and Malt Wine' were both advertised. The firm used to collect doctors' prescriptions and deliver the medicines to your house. Today Ryman are suppliers of office stationery.

This parade of shops between Anselm Road and Racton Road, seen here in about 1913, has been completely rebuilt. A donkey cart is making its way along the busy road, filled with people eager to snap up the latest bargains from the market stalls.

North End Road, *c.* 1913. It looks very similar today with its market stalls set out on the eastern side of the road. Epirus Road is to the left and Eustace Road is on the right. The block on the right was Barber's department store, which closed in the 1990s. Frederick H. Barber opened his draper's shop in 1891 and over the years the store was rebuilt and expanded to occupy the entire block from Eustace Road to Armadale Road.

Fulham Streets

An early motor car awaits its passengers in Mirabel Road, 1913. The road was developed in 1886. In the distance is Dawes Road.

Adeney Street, *c.* 1909. This view is now impossible to reproduce as Adeney Street and several neighbouring streets were demolished in the 1970s to make way for the erection, by the Greater London Council, of the Bayonne Road housing estate. The earlier view was taken from the corner of Lillie Road and Everington Street, where a blank wall would greet today's visitor. The modern view is of Adeney Close, taken from Delorme Street.

Alderville Road, viewed from New Kings Road, *c.* 1914. Hurlingham Park is at the far end.

Armadale Road, viewed from North End Road, *c.* 1913. The grandly named International School of Motoring, occupying the premises at the far end of the road, also offered cars for hire. The houses on the right have been demolished to make way for the enlargement of a store on North End Road.

Bishops Road, at the junction with Rostrevor Road, *c.* 1914. Only two houses on the left have retained the gable ends on the roofline. The small corner shops, which acted like a magnet to all those children, have closed. The one on the right housed a computer systems supplier for a time but now lies empty. Filmer Road is to the left.

Looking south from New Kings Road along Broomhouse Road, *c.* 1914. A new development on the left includes the introduction of house fronts that duplicate the appearance of the existing houses. The first two houses on the right have lost their wooden railings on the small balconies but one has retained the tall doors that led out on to the balcony.

Crabtree Lane, *c.* 1914. The road here was little more than a gravel track leading down to the River Thames. Until the late 1890s the land hereabouts, off Fulham Palace Road, was mainly used for market gardens, with strawberries and cabbages still being grown in about 1909. Clifford Haigh House has been built on the former church site on the left, on the corner of Fulham Palace Road.

De Morgan Road, viewed from Stephendale Road, *c.* 1925. Van Den Bergh's margarine factory is at the southern end. The factory functioned here from the end of the nineteenth century until 1934 when it closed. The factory building survives, albeit in a derelict condition. The terraced houses on the right have all been demolished and replaced by the local authority Townmead housing estate. William de Morgan's pottery was founded in 1888 in Townmead Road, manufacturing a range of tiles to combat the dirt and corrosive nature of London's atmosphere.

The Baptist Chapel, Twynholm, at Fulham Cross, Lillie Road, *c.* 1908. The chapel today has more of an ecclesiastical appearance. In 1908 the ground floor was occupied by Lockhart's Dining Rooms, where a large mug of tea would set you back a penny and a steak pudding cost 4½*d*. The premises promoted themselves as the 'Best in London'.

Munster Road at the junction with Dawes Road, *c.* 1912. In the background is Twynholm at Fulham Cross. This building was intended as a public house but was taken up in 1893 by the evangelist Sydney Black as a Baptist mission chapel. The gap in the parade next to Munster Tyres has been sympathetically filled in with a matching building. The two-storey terraced houses have lost their gardens and had shop fronts added.

A horse-drawn van belonging to J. & T.H. Wallis, of the Wandle Flour Mills at Beddington in Surrey, is making a delivery in Kenyon Street in 1906/7. All the traffic in the road is concerned with the delivery of household items. Laundry, fish, milk, dairy products and bread were delivered on a daily basis as housewives were not usually in employment and were available at home to receive the goods. Refrigeration was not common in most households at that time and perishable items could not be stored for lengthy periods.

Munster Road viewed from Fulham Cross, *c.* 1908. The five two-storey houses on the left have been converted into shops. Today this area seems to be almost entirely made up of antiques shops and second-hand shops. The Fulham Cross Dairy is now the Bathroom Discount Centre. The oil jars above the shop on the left were fairly common until the late 1960s and denoted the whereabouts of oil and colour stores. These were mainly ironmongers that would also mix up paint colours. They also sold paraffin and a thousand small items for the home.

In 1914 St Dionis Road was still called Rectory Road after the parish church rectory that stood facing Parsons Green. The ancient rectory, dating from 1707, was last in use as a military academy and was demolished in 1882 for the building of St Dionis Church. The building opposite the church is the mission hall with the Jolly Brewers public house next door. The corner shop, grandly named Guion House, is now used as offices. Guion Road is on the right.

Rigault Road, viewed from Landridge Road, *c*. 1914. Rigault Road contains the remains of the Fulham Refuge for Women. In 1855 the government had purchased the former Burlington Academy in Burlington Road for the construction of a women's prison. The prison was closed in 1888 and sold off in 1893. The majority of the buildings were demolished over the years to make way for housing development but what appears to have been the prison laundry survives today as the Burlington Lodge Studios on the corner of Buer Road.

Settringham Street, from Clancarty Road, *c.* 1913. The double twist in this street is difficult to photograph today. The trees had not been planted in the earlier photograph.

Shorrolds Road, from Dawes Road, *c.* 1914. North End Road can be seen at the far end and Fabian Road is on the left, just beyond the two girls in the earlier scene.

Hammersmith

St Paul's parish church at Hammersmith, *c.* 1913. The first church in use for the residents of Hammersmith was All Saints', Fulham's parish church, but Hammersmith residents petitioned the Bishop of London for permission to build their own church, and this was granted in 1629. The church was consecrated on 7 June 1631. By the nineteenth century it was inadequate for the ever-increasing population and it was rebuilt in its present form, with its 157 ft tower, in 1883. With the construction of the A4 Hammersmith flyover and the recent Broadway developments, the church is now overshadowed and partly obscured.

Hammersmith Bridge, viewed from Barnes, *c.* 1914. Across the river is the City Arms public house; the date of 1898 on the building is much later than it deserves. The pub has been rebuilt and is now in use as offices. Hammersmith's first bridge across the Thames was opened in 1827. It was replaced by the present structure, designed by Sir Joseph Bazalgette, in 1887. The IRA attempted to blow up the bridge in 1939 and again more recently.

The approach to Hammersmith Bridge, *c.* 1925. Digby Mansions, on the right, were built in about 1900, replacing some small eighteenth-century houses.

The Mall, viewed from Hammersmith Bridge, *c.* 1912. The grandstand on the roof of the Rutland Hotel is plainly visible. The houses here have survived from the eighteenth century, and no. 6 is the headquarters of the Amateur Rowing Association. Kent House at no. 10 was built in about 1762 and is owned by the Hammersmith Club Society. The rowing skiffs are no longer moored here. They used to be popular for hiring for an early morning row on the river as a means of exercise before leaving for work.

The Rutland Hotel dates from 1880. It once sported a viewing platform on the roof to admire the boat racing but this, together with the top floor, was lost to wartime bombing. The Anchor public house is just two doors further along the Mall, by the trees. The West End Rowing Association Club boathouse, on the left, has been demolished and replaced by a small block of flats.

The Mall, viewed from Hammersmith Bridge, *c.* 1914. The major alterations today include the removal of the chimneys from the West Middlesex Waterworks and the Albert Mills, both now closed. The *Stork* training ship can be seen in front of the chimneys, at its mooring at Hammersmith. The *Stork* was built in 1850 as a naval gunboat. She retired from active service and was converted into a training ship by the Navy League in 1912. She was moored here until 1948 and broken up two years later.

The earlier Hammersmith station, seen here in about 1914, was in the Broadway, almost opposite Shepherds Bush Road. The station was built in 1874 for the District Railway but also had in its title the Great Northern Piccadilly & Brompton Railway, which ran its line at a greater depth. The station was sadly demolished in about 1990 to make way for the Brodero Broadway development scheme. A new station was built into the façade of the new Broadway Shopping Centre, now almost facing King Street.

The old and the new Underground stations, *c.* 1914 and 2002. Modern traffic management schemes in Hammersmith bunch the traffic together and long lines of vehicles clutter up the views for some time, making it very difficult to take photographs today. Recently planted trees alongside the station also help to obscure the landscape.

The Broadway and Queen Caroline Street, *c.* 1914. Palmer's department store occupies the corner position on King Street and Queen Caroline Street. This popular store, founded in 1886, closed in the 1950s and the building was demolished in the 1980s. In its place at 1–15 King Street is the West London Corporate and Business Centre of the National Westminster Bank. The five-storey building at 2 Queen Caroline Street, on the corner of Blacks Road, now houses Bar 38 on the ground floor and offices above.

The old Hammersmith Town Hall, seen here in about 1914, had a wonderful 'wedding cake' tower that was lost when the building was demolished in the 1960s. Traffic movement in the area today is poor, with delays built into traffic light sequencing and bus lanes imposed on the local streets.

Hammersmith Broadway, *c.* 1925. In the background, in what was then Brook Green Road, stands the Town Hall. Demolished in the 1960s, it has been replaced by two office blocks; the one on the right is let out to Iberia Airways and is more pleasing to look at than the rather plain five-storey block alongside. In the earlier scene two efficient-looking policemen on point duty are directing the traffic, horse-drawn and mechanical.

Two public houses help us to get our bearings in these views of the Broadway from the Hammersmith Road in 1914 and 2002. The George public house on the right has hardly been altered in the intervening years. The Bovril sign in the earlier scene is on the upper façade of the Swan pub, now Edward's, on the corner of King Street.

One of four railway stations to bear the name Hammersmith, this one was opened in 1868 on the Metropolitan line. The Great Western Railway had a partnership in the running of the station. The earlier view is from about 1911 and shows a number of men selling flowers on the forecourt. There are advertisements for tickets to the Cheltenham races – try booking tickets for Cheltenham today at this station! The canopy has since been removed, together with all references to the previous railway companies. The misnamed Transport for London is now in control of the London Underground railway system.

King Street, *c.* 1914. During the Kings Mall shopping centre development of the 1970s, which resulted in the demolition of all the small shops seen here, a proviso was made that the auditorium of the old Lyric Theatre was to be incorporated into the new theatre. Her Majesty Queen Elizabeth II opened the new Lyric Theatre on 18 October 1979. It occupies the taller part of the development near Beadon Road on the left.

King Street, seen from opposite Holcombe Street, facing east, *c.* 1914. The Electric Palace cinema stood two doors along from Macbeth Street. It has been replaced with a three-storey office block named Appleton House. Next door to the cinema is the Penny Farthing public house, presently (August 2002) undergoing refurbishment. The London Borough of Fulham and Hammersmith social services department occupies the ground floor of the modern five-storey block on the right.

A summer's day in King Street, *c.* 1914, and the street is full of people and delivery carts. The Hammersmith Ram public house on the right, on the corner of Angel Walk, has a cast-iron milestone set against the wall which states 'Hammersmith Parish Hounslow 6½ London 3½'. The local authority Ashmore Square flats above the Kings Mall shopping centre are more easily seen in this view.

King Street, 1922. The department store on the corner of Bridge Avenue, on the right, is advertising winter clothing for the coming season. The Halifax Building Society now occupies the site. The pub sign of the Hammersmith Ram, on the corner of Angel Walk, can just be seen in the modern view. The shops beyond the pub have been rebuilt. A Primark store and the Kings Mall shopping centre have replaced the shops on the left.

King Street, with Bridge Avenue on the left, *c.* 1925. On the right is the Hammersmith Palace of Varieties music hall. Originally a theatre attached to the Town Hall Tavern, it was rebuilt in 1898 with 2,815 seats to the designs of the architect W.M. Brutton. The theatre attracted music hall stars such as Dan Leno, Marie Lloyd and Vesta Tillie. It was converted for cinema use in 1931 but was badly damaged by bombing in 1944 and was demolished in 1950. On the right of the picture below is part of the Kings Mall shopping centre with the Ashmore Square residential flats above.

Historians would love to be able to go back to 1914 and purchase some of the postcard views on display in the window of Fordham's stationers, confectioners and sub-post office at 323 King Street. These late eighteenth- and early nineteenth-century shops have been demolished and replaced by a local authority high-rise block of flats called Standish House; the petrol station now stands empty awaiting new proprietors. St Peter's Grove is to the right and Standish Road is further along. The sub-post office has been moved a little further along King Street to no. 353 and the street has been renumbered along the south side.

King Street, with Ravenscourt Road on the left, *c.* 1914. The corner shop at no. 230 looks a little bland today compared with the numerous signs put up by the estate agents and auctioneers James Chamberlen in the earlier view. The cottages on the left, probably dating from the eighteenth century, are remarkable survivors. The only major alteration has been the insertion of plate glass windows to some of the shop fronts, rather spoiling the character of the buildings.

King Street, with Weltje Road on the right, *c.* 1936. Dependability House, on the right, formerly Wiggins & Sankey builders merchants, is in use as offices for Upper Latymer School next door. The tall spire of Riverscourt Methodist church can be seen through the trees. Out of sight, to the right, in front of Pallingswick House, is a drinking fountain erected in 1887 to the memory of S.L. Swabb Esq. It is inscribed: 'His knowledge like a spring of refreshing water flowed ever during life for the relief of suffering.'

King Street, *c.* 1914. The Plough and Harrow public house on the left was converted in the 1950s into showrooms selling Rolls-Royce cars. A recent development has seen a Holiday Inn hotel built to the rear of the premises. The pub group Wetherspoon's is converting (August 2002) the ground floor back into a public house, which will bear the original name of the Plough and Harrow. Macbeth Street is to the right.

Hammersmith Road, from near the corner of Shepherds Bush Road, *c.* 1914. On the left is the Sacred Heart School for Girls. This was the site of the Sacred Heart convent, which was set up in the time of Charles II and survived until 1863. The site was in use by several Catholic communities and was rebuilt in its present form in 1876. The girls' school was started in 1893. Overlarge office blocks, with tenants including L'Oreal cosmetics and Bechtel, have appeared along Hammersmith Road, and road widening schemes have destroyed such places as the Clarendon Restaurant on the right, where afternoon teas were once served.

The façade of the former West London Hospital has been cleaned and refurbished and the building now houses the offices of Sony Ericsson. The main hospital buildings have been demolished and replaced with offices and flats. The former nurses' building, Abercorn Home, built in 1917 in Bute Gardens to the left, is now a Youth Hostel. The West London Hospital was founded on the site of the former Elm Tree House in the 1860s and eventually became a teaching hospital. It was closed in the 1980s during the reorganisation of London hospitals. Of interest is the small drinking fountain, now dry, set into the railings on the corner of Bute Gardens: it bears no dedication or explanation for its existence.

St Peter's Church in St Peter's Square was built in 1829 to the designs of Edward Lapidge, before the surrounding development of the square. The view is from Black Lion Lane, which has been cut in two by the construction of the six-lane A4 Great West Road. The small eighteenth-century building on the right has been demolished and replaced by the Samels Court private housing estate.

Bridge Avenue, *c.* 1914, with an unrestricted view all the way up to King Street. This was altered in the late 1950s and early 1960s with the construction of the Hammersmith flyover on the A4 Great West Road, which cut this street in two, destroying several properties in the process. The modern view was taken from Rutland Grove and appears dark in the distance owing to the flyover beyond the line of vehicles. King Street can just be seen at the far end.

Coulter Road, viewed from Ifley Road, *c.* 1914. Nos 8–28 are shown, with Tabor Road at the far end.

Ravenscourt Park, formerly the private grounds to Ravenscourt House. The area was first mentioned in the thirteenth century as Palingswick Green. The Stamford Brook fed the moat surrounding the manor house. The house was called Paddenswick until it was renamed in 1765 by Thomas Corbett. He transformed the moat into the lake that still survives in part today. As well as Canada geese the lake is home to moorhens, mandarin ducks, coots, mute swans and mallard, pochard and tufted ducks. The park was opened to the public in 1888 and the house became a public library. Sadly it was destroyed in the Second World War.

Shepherds Bush

The magnificently decorated main entrance to the White City Exhibition Centre on the Uxbridge Road at Shepherds Bush, *c.* 1928. The halls were opened in 1908 with the Franco-British Exhibition, followed in 1909 by the Imperial Exhibition; 1910 saw the Japan British Exhibition and 1911 the Coronation Exhibition. The last show before the First World War was the Anglo-American Exhibition of 1914. The government took over the site for training troops and part of it was used for the manufacture of materials for the forces. Several small exhibitions were held here in the 1920s and 1930s but it was soon superseded by the nearby Olympia show halls. Most of the grounds have been built on, with housing, the BBC Television Centre and new roadways, and the site has been earmarked for development for several years.

The short section of road between the Broadway at Hammersmith and Brook Green was called Brook Green Road in 1911 but it was renamed Shepherds Bush Road on 1 June 1968 to blend in with the rest of the length of Shepherds Bush Road from Brook Green northwards. On the left is Hammersmith Library, opened in 1905. Beyond the tram is the old Town Hall which was built in 1897 and survived until demolition in 1965. It was replaced with office blocks.

Shepherds Bush Road, *c.* 1914. Brook Green lies on both sides of the road. The Brook Green Hotel was built in 1886 and was leased to the brewers Young & Co. in 1888. The pub's Victorian decor was refurbished in about 1990, bringing back to life its decorated ceilings and glasswork. The house and shop next door at 168 Shepherds Bush Road were incorporated into the pub in 1983.

Shepherds Bush Road near the corner of Brook Green, *c.* 1919. During rebuilding and renovation works in about 1978 on two shops, nos 152 and 154 on the left, the central party wall collapsed bringing down both properties. Both premises had to be rebuilt.

Shepherds Bush Road from the corner of Poplar Grove, *c.* 1911. In the background, beyond the tram, is the Methodist chapel on the corner of Netherwood Road and Blythe Road. Now demolished, it has been replaced by Baradell House flats. The terrace on the left has been given over mainly to guesthouses and small hotels.

The White City Exhibition entrance on Uxbridge Road, *c.* 1920. The exhibition centre was the brainchild of the Hungarian Imre Kiralfy. The site covered 200 acres between Uxbridge Road and Wood Lane and up to where the A40 road now runs. The first event was the Franco-British Exhibition of 1908 that coincided with the holding of the Olympic Games. Almost 8½ million people were to visit the site in 1908. The exhibition entrance, minus its wonderful decoration, is now in use by the gaming company City Paint Ball Co. and the remaining exhibition halls are used for storage.

Uxbridge Road station on the West London Railway, *c*. 1914. The station was opened in November 1893. The line was closed to passenger traffic in October 1940 but the platforms here survived into the 1960s. The station entrance was eventually demolished in about 1971 for road widening at the entrance to the West Cross Route that leads to the A40 Westway road. The Mailcoach Inn, rebuilt in the 1930s, no longer enjoys the huge clientele it had when the White City exhibitions were in full swing. The glass tower on the right in the modern scene is part of the Thames Water Ring Main installed in the 1980s. It is one of eleven pumping shafts spread throughout London along the 80km tunnel.

The Uxbridge Road at Shepherds Bush, *c.* 1914. Note the J. Lyons' cornerhouse tea-rooms on the corner of Shepherds Bush Place. This parade of shops was erected in 1908. The cornerhouse is now a Budgen's 24-hour convenience store and supermarket. Shepherds Bush Green is to the left.

The shopping parade on the Uxbridge Road, opposite the green, *c.* 1920. The Board of Trade Labour Exchange is on the right, with a cinema next door. The cinema is now a Superdrug store and the Labour Exchange is a McDonald's fast food outlet with the Slug and Lettuce public house nearby. The parade of seven outlets, including the pub, was built in 1905.

The corner of Wood Lane and Uxbridge Road, *c.* 1916. The Beaumont Arms public house, originally dating from the early nineteenth century, was rebuilt at the end of the century as seen here. It has recently been renamed Edward's bar. Three doors along from the pub was the Star Cinema, advertising 'Continuous Performances'; this meant shows went on throughout the afternoon and into the evening.

The Bush Hotel public house on the corner of Goldhawk Road, now renamed O'Neill's, stands on what was, until the 1890s, the site of the White Horse Brewery. The Bush Theatre was opened in 1972 in a small room above the pub. To the right is the Shepherds Bush Empire Music Hall, built by Sir Oswald Stoll in 1903 for an audience of 2,332. It was taken over by the BBC in 1953 as its television theatre. The building remained empty for a number of years in the 1980s but in 1993 it was refurbished to hold pop concerts. Mark Knopfler was appearing here in July 2002.

The Pavilion cinema was opened in August 1923, with seating for 2,767. Seen here in about 1925, the building took a direct hit from a V1 doodlebug in 1944 but it only suffered some small damage at this northern end and was soon repaired. The cinema underwent a series of name changes, to the Gaumont in 1955 and then the Odeon in 1962. It closed in 1969 and reopened in 1970 as a cinema with 850 seats and as a bingo hall. The cinema section, in the former circle, finally closed in 1983. Its use for bingo lasted a few more years but the building was boarded up in 2001. There are plans for it to be used for entertainment allied to a pub chain. The terrace of houses on the right has been replaced by the Threshold House office block, which is rented by the BBC.

The Walkabout Australian Bar was built in 1910 as a Pyke's circuit cinema and was renamed the Palladium in about 1923. It is seen here in about 1925. It was renamed the Essoldo in 1955, the Classic in 1972 and finally the Odeon in 1973. It closed as a cinema in 1981 and was left derelict for some years before conversion into a public house. On the exterior wall a notice in a cement panel reads: 'Cinematograph Theatre – Continuous Performance – Seats 1*s*, 6*d* & 3*d*' in letters about 4 ft high. The larger building next door is the Pavilion Cinema.

Camerer Kuss & Co., watchmakers and jewellers, at 186 Uxbridge Road, c. 1913. The business was founded by a German immigrant at the beginning of the nineteenth century. At the commencement of the First World War great hostility was shown to anyone with a German-sounding title and the firm decided to alter its name to Camerer Cuss, dropping the K. They even placed advertisements in local newspapers insisting that they were British subjects.

Uxbridge Road, with Oaklands Grove on the right, *c.* 1914. The turreted building is the Queen Adelaide public house, on the corner of Adelaide Grove. The scene has altered very little except for the addition of a shop front to the corner house on the right.

A 1936 Lincoln Zephyr V16 making its way to Shepherds Bush along Goldhawk Road, *c.* 1938. The former bank at nos 39–41, on the corner of Woodger Road on the left, is now Hecht & Co. solicitors office. The larger building on the left is Goldhawk House, built in 1903. Enamel signs placed high up on the wall still proclaim 'Wallpapers – Builders Ironmongery – Colours, Glass &C', although the building is now a Europa food and wine store and supermarket.

The parade of shops, nos 104–86, in Goldhawk Road, *c.* 1935. Devonport Road is on the left and Hammersmith Grove is opposite.

The Railway Arms public house in Goldhawk Road, at the entrance to Shepherds Bush market, has been converted into a shop. Back in 1914 the pub must have done a roaring trade, situated alongside the market. The rest of the parade has lost the rendered drip sill near the roof line, one shop has had its windows boarded up and the brickwork of the entire parade has been rendered over, spoiling the general appearance.

The Wheatsheaf public house on the corner of Goldhawk Road and Brackenbury Road, *c.* 1914. The wrought-iron bracket above the entrance remains but without the original pub name and street number as the pub has been renamed the Brackenbury Arms and the property renumbered from 189 to 163 Goldhawk Road.

Goldhawk Road, *c.* 1914. On the left is the Shepherd and Flock public house, on the corner of Titmus Square; it is aptly named as it's only a short distance from Shepherds Bush Green.

The enamel signs high on the wall of Goldhawk House in Goldhawk Road are noticeable in both views of *c.* 1914 and 2002. Some confusion must have reigned here as on the corner of Wells Road, on the right, is the Railway Tavern public house, which stood opposite the Railway Arms public house (*see* p. 110). The Railway Tavern has been renamed the Bushranger bar.

Dalling Road, at the corner of Glenthorne Road, *c.* 1914. The man on the left is carrying out a jug of ale from the off-licence; this was a common method of retailing beer before the Second World War. Further along on the left is the Prince of Wales public house, rebuilt in the 1930s. Renamed Tommy Flynn's, it is presently undergoing refurbishment and enlargement. The former off-licence at no. 57 is now Butler & Lawler's hairdressing salon. Most of the shops here are now private houses and screened off from the public. The second block of shops on the right is seen on the next page.

Dalling Road, *c.* 1914. These late nineteenth-century shops between Redmore Road and Raynham Road have all been demolished and houses erected in their place. The houses have retained the original street numbering, 68–86 Dalling Road. In 1914 the parade of shops included oil stores, a post and telegraph office, a fish and chip shop, a grocers, a clothing shop and, at no. 88, R. Barnard's removals and second-hand furniture store.

The enamel sign for the Kings Parade on the corner of Askew Road and Goldhawk Road has survived but how many people still use the name for this parade of shops? To the left is Starch Green, probably the smallest park in Hammersmith. An early reference occurs in 1397 when it was called Stork's Green, possibly named after a tenant farmer of that name. The properties on the left, seen here in about 1914, have all been demolished and local authority housing named Kelmscott Gardens erected in their place.

The Eagle public house in Askew Road, *c*. 1914 and 2002. The tramlines have gone, the cast-iron railings have been removed from the property to the left and the three empty shops on the right have been let for many years but otherwise hardly a thing has changed in these two views, taken eighty-five years apart.

Conningham Road, *c.* 1914. Only a few pedestrians, a coal delivery cart and a small hand-pushed dairy cart are in view. The properties have hardly been altered over the years except for the disappearance of the garden railings in 1940–1 for the wartime scrap drive.

Glenthorne Road, *c.* 1914. The shops on the left have all been demolished to make way for the construction of the Kings Mall multi-storey car park. The whole terrace of houses on the right, from Overstone Road to Southerton Road, has been taken over by the Premier West Hotel. St John the Evangelist Church, now hidden by the trees, was designed by William Butterfield and consecrated in 1859.

Greenside Road, *c*. 1914. On the right is the Presbyterian Church of St Andrew, which has been rededicated by the Polish community to St Andrew Bobola, a Jesuit priest who was tortured and murdered by the Cossacks on 16 May 1657. He was canonised on 16 May 1957 and his feast day is 23 May.

North Pole Road, at the corner of Wood Lane, 1908. The road was laid out by the military in 1812 when the government took over Wormwood Scrubbs for military manoeuvres; it was then called Turwens Lane. The Pavilion Hotel was reconstructed in 1896 and has been altered again since. In 1904 it had a concert hall and billiards room. Alongside the railway bridge in the background was the St Quintin and Wormwood Scrubbs railway station. Opened in November 1893, it was destroyed in a fire-bomb attack on 3 October 1940.

Redan Street, viewed from Masbro Road, *c.* 1914. The children in the middle of the road are doubtless wondering what to do next. The small shop on the corner of Spring Terrace, on the left, is now a private house. In the background is Addison Primary School in Bolingbroke Road.

Lime Grove, *c.* 1925. The White Horse public house on the corner of Uxbridge Road has given most of its ground floor over to Blockbuster Video. Next to the pub entrance on Uxbridge Road is a milestone embedded in the wall that states 'Hammersmith Parish – London III Miles – Uxbridge XII Miles'. On the western side of Lime Grove are the Hammersmith public baths and wash-houses, built in 1908, and next door the Hammersmith and West London College. Lime Grove was famous for the BBC Television studios, in use from 1950 until 1960, when the new television centre was opened in Wood Lane. The studios were built in 1913 for film production, and Rank, Gaumont British and Gainsborough films were made here.

Stamford Brook Road, *c.* 1914. On the right is St Mary's Church, opened in 1886 to the designs of Charles J. Gladman. The church has been converted into flats called St Mary's Court. The Vicarage, on the other side of Flanchford Road (beyond the girls on the right), has also been converted into living accommodation. Stamford Brook derives its name from a stony ford across the river where the old Roman road, now Goldhawk Road, met the stream. The water is now channelled underground.

The Author & Local History Sources

Patrick Loobey was born in 1947. He joined the Wandsworth Historical Society (founded in 1953) in 1969 and has served on its archaeological, publication and management committees. He was chairman from 1991 to 1994 and from 1998 to 2001. Having collected Edwardian postcards and photographs of south-west London for thirty years, he now has a wide-ranging collection of about 40,000 pictures illustrating many local roads and subjects.

Hammersmith & Fulham Past & Present complements other recent books by Patrick, notably *Putney Past & Present* (2001), *Wimbledon Past & Present* (2002), *Streatham Past & Present* (2001), *Streatham: The Twentieth Century* (2000) and various titles on Battersea and Clapham, Balham and Tooting, Wandsworth and others.

The captions to the photographs in this book offer a brief glimpse into the varied and complex history of the area. For those seeking further information, the Fulham and Hammersmith Historical Society holds a series of meetings and lectures throughout the year, and also publishes a range of books on local history. It can be contacted via the Hammersmith and Fulham Archives and Local History Collection at The Lilla Huset, 191 Talgarth Road, London W6 8BJ. Tel: 020 8741 5159. The archives department contains a wealth of historical material on the area's history and is very helpful to those seeking information on family and commercial connections.